P O E M S

ON

SEVERAL OCCASIONS.

PRINTED AT STOKE PARK, 1802.

CONTENTS.

Addressed to JOHN PENN, *Esq.*

Go! humble Lays, go, and with truth impart,
The secret sufferings of a sorrowing Heart;
Tell how in silent anguish long I grieved,
Tell with what woes this hapless bosom heaved,
Till by the aid of Friendship's potent balm,
My troubled Soul enjoys its present calm.

MARY PYE.

MAD SONG.

WITH down-cast Eye, and solemn pace,
   Poor ELLEN wanders o'er the plain,
Her Locks unbound, and pale her face;
   Sad Victim to love's slighted pain.

Lost are her wits; her reason lost:
   No tear she sheds, no word she speaks:
Deceived by him she trusted most,
   With silent grief her sad Heart breaks.

Warm was her Heart for others' grief,
   Tho' now in Icy Fetters bound;
And if a sufferer sought relief,
   Pity in ELLEN's breast they found.

Her Eyes, which once, with brightest beam,
   Expressive shone on all around,
Are fix'd on vacancy; or gleam,
   With frenzied torpor, on the ground.

Her Voice! whose soft and dulcet sound
   Charm'd ev'ry ear with pure delight,
Is now in death-like silence bound;
   And sunk in never ending night.

This wreck of genius, worth, and grace,
   Ah! faithless Man, draw near and see:
Nought can her senses e'er replace;
   Victim, to Sorrow, Love, and Thee.

TO MISFORTUNE.

O! there's a Charm in that dejected Eye;
O! there's more danger, in that deep-drawn sigh,
Than in the playful wiles of sportive wit,
When happy laughter, and the graces sit
Thron'd with gay pleasure, on the brow of youth;
O! there's more peril in misfortune's sigh,
More to be dreaded from the tearful Eye
Telling the Sufferer's misery with truth.—
When sunshine round the head of affluence flings,
Its rays, it every idle Insect brings,
Buzzing around in Fortune's cheerful hour;
But when the clouds of Poverty o'er-spread,
Mark! and thou'lt find, the fickle swarms are fled;
Fled to some brighter, sweeter, richer Flower!—
Not so with One true Heart, misfortune's chain
Has hopeless bound, in never-ending pain.
Had'st thou been happy, I had still been free,—
Thy adverse Fortune made a slave of me.

DESPAIR.

[4]

DESPAIR.

O! Stranger, dos't thou ask me why
This down-cast look, this heaving sigh?
Why from my cheeks the rose is gone?
Why from my lip the smile is flown.?
O! Stranger, seek thou not to know
The cause of my Soul-piercing woe?
'Twould only rend thy feeling *Heart*,
And no relief to *mine* impart;
For what avails soft pity's sigh,
Or what avails the moisten'd Eye,
To her who every Hope has lost,
Chill'd by despair's keen-biting frost?—
She who in absence mourns her Love
The anguish of suspense must prove;
But still Creative Hope portrays
Fair prospects of some happier days;
Not so with me; for round my head
The wreath of *Hope* is wither'd—dead.

10

TO HOPE.

HOPE, blessed hope, oh never leave my Heart,
Still with thy witching smiles new joys impart ;
Still round my brow thy blooming wreath entwine,
And tho' thou oft deceiv'st, O ! still be mine.—
Ah ! blessed Hope, fair Hope of happier hours,
Strew in my path thy never-fading flowers ;
Still let Imagination's pencil gay
Dipp'd in bright tints some distant bliss portray ;
Telling in future days there's peace in store
When this sad sorrowing Heart shall sigh no more.
But if at last thou provest an empty dream,
If on my future fate no sunbeams gleam,
In happy ignorance still keep me blest,
Nor cloud the present sun-shine of my Breast.

SONG.

SONG.

HAVE you not seen a sweet, an early flower
Expand its buds and raise its dewy head ?
Have you not seen a cold, a chilling shower
Wither each Leaf, and all its blossoms shed ?

So the young heart when fann'd by Hope's soft
        breeze,
Expands its folds to catch affection's breath ;
But cold neglect will soon each blossom freeze,
Blight every Leaf, and sink its bloom in Death.

ON

ON MY BIRTHDAY.

SEE not one smiling bud unfold this Morn,
Each dew-drop frozen on the leafless Thorn,
Emblem of her whose every hope is gone,
Whose every cheering ray of comfort s flown.
Alas! how chang'd *this Day*, ere-while so blest,
When not one racking care disturb'd my rest,
When no corrosive anguish fill'd my mind,
And every joy to hail it was combin'd.
No more joy's sparkling ray illumes mine Eyes;
My Bosom heav'd with deep, with ceaseless sighs,
Amidst surrounding revelry I'm sad;
Nought now can charm, nor aught can make me
    glad;
But tho' no longer my poor Heart can know
A touch of pleasure (fraught alas! with woe,)
Reflected joys I from my Friends will steal,
The only sun-shine this sad Heart can feel.

ANSWER

ANSWER BY H. I. PYE.

DEAR Mary, why the pensive lays
That usher in thy natal morn, ?
Sill shall the light of happier days
Thy hours with brilliant tint adorn.

Tho' Fortune's inauspicious breeze
Oppose a while thy fleeting sails,
Soon shall thy Bark thro' summer seas
Be wafted by the favouring gales.

Nor Summer seas, nor favouring gale
Can on my shatter'd Vessel wait :
Impell'd by Time, my tatter'd sail
Spreads onward to the gulf of Fate.

Yet unapall'd by waves and wind,
Forward I steer my destin'd course;
Secure the unconquerable Mind
Can brave the Tempest's fiercest force.

Certain that on this shoal of Time
Alternate Suns and Clouds must rise,
Patient I wait the happier clime,
When ceaseless radiance lights the skies.

ANSWERED.

ANSWERED.

THINK not 'twas Fortune's frown that caus'd my
    lays,
For she might frown, might sternly frown in vain.
'Twas not her clouded brow, that dimm'd my rays;
Or caus'd the heaving sigh, the bitter pain.

For witness Heaven, and O! be witness Earth,
No one privation Fortune harshly dealt
Could for a moment have depress'd my mirth,
Or in my bosom have been keenly felt.

But there are pangs more keen then Fortune's loss,
More freezing far than penury's chill wind,
When warring passions still on passions toss,
Whelming the Soul, and over-come the Mind.

Those happy hours describ'd can ne'er return;
No more this aching Heart to joy can wake.
On Earth, I must forever, ever mourn;
But Hope this bosom never shall forsake.

Hope of a better World where pain no more
Shall hold Dominion o'er this tortur'd Breast;
When I those happy regions may explore,
And in the Bosom of my God shall rest.

C   TO

TO A YOUNG LADY,

On her Birthday, and seeing her surrounded by her Family.

I

SWEET flower of June, ah may no chilling blast
Blight the fair promise of thy opening bloom!
May every year a livelier charm bestow,
And no dark vapour spoil thy rich perfume!

Long mayst thou blossom 'neath the Parent plant!
Long flourish fair amidst thy sister flowers!
Ah! may no canker worm thy folds invade,
To wound thy leaves and chill thy passing hours!

Such is the wish of Friendship; tho' alas!
That wish perchance will unavailing flow:
For frail Mortality is doom'd to fade;
And we are all the certain Heirs of woe.

But when within the Breast firm Virtue glows,
The Blast of Sorrow we may bravely dare.
Tho for awhile it withers every Leaf,
Yet they'll revive and bloom, more sweet, more
fair.

TO MY SISTER ON HER BIRTHDAY.

MAIDENS go forth, go pluck each floweret fair
And form a *wreath* to deck my sister's hair;
The Rose, the Lily pure, the pink so gay,
To grace her brow on this her Natal Day.
Alas! I quite forgot November's gloom
Has now despoil'd them of thir lovely bloom.
That not one opening bud will now unfold,
Nor one green leaf our sorrowing Eyes behold.
Yet tho' they all refuse their aid to lend,
To help this trifling tribute of a Friend;
Know then that on this blest auspicious day
A *wreath* I'll form whose sweets shall rival May.
See on Matilda's cheek the blushing rose
And her pure breast the Lily will disclose;
While o'er *my wreath*, fair Virtue's soft perfume
Sheds its sweet breath and bids it ever bloom.

SONG.

SONG.

WHEN forced to part from those we Love
Tho' sure to meet to morrow ;
We still a kind of anguish prove
And feel a touch of sorrow.

But Oh ! what words can paint the tears
We shed, as thus we sever,
When doom'd to part for Months, for Years—
Perhaps to part forever ?

THE

THE WITHER'D ROSE.

MARK yon sad Rose once summer's darling
    pride,
That threw its blooming odours far and wide,
Now all its bright, its blushing honors past;
Too dazzling fair alas! and sweet to last.
But yet tho' scatter'd be each silken Leaf
By cruel Time, that sad despoiling Thief,
Still from those Leaves exhale a rich perfume;
Still they are sweet tho' they have ceas'd to bloom.
So lov'd Remembrances of joys long fled
O'er the sad Heart their soothing influence shed:
While in the Breast is saved each wither'd Leaf
Of past delight,—to sooth its present grief.

SONNET 10. THE NIGHTSHADE.

Oh! beauteous weed, expanding every fold,
To catch the breath of morn begemm'd with dew,
Thy opening buds so lovely to behold,
Steal o'er the sense, and fascinate the view.
But oh! be warn'd! nor idly venture there.
Touch not a Leaf, but from it quickly fly;
For 'neath those silken leaves so tempting fair,
Poison there lurks.—Who tastes must surely die.
So from the smiling Flowers of treacherous Love
Poor fond declining maids no ills suspect,
Till ah! too fatally alas they'd prove
The poisonous chalice of severe neglect.
No solace can for cold neglect be found:
Deep is the sting; incurable the wound.

ON PLEASURE.

O! glittering Pleasure, in thy splendid ray
Pangs oft assail us while thy sun-beams play.
E'en while their cheering influence glads the
    Heart
Sorrow's fell poison barbs the fated Dart,
To wound our peace forever with some grief
Unalterable, and without relief.
E'en while alas, the sad, the sorrowing breast
Enjoys a soothing calm, a transient rest,
Springs some new wretchedness, some sudden ill,
With tenfold anguish each sad heart to fill.
Pleasure avaunt, thou ne'er shalt cheat me more;
Thy flitting Phantom-charms for me are o'er.
I've found thy smiles were only to deceive,
And with redoubled anguish make me grieve.
Like *Thee* I've seen the cheating morning hour
Wake into Life some sweet and tender flower;
Soon have I seen dark clouds o'ercast the skies,
Or some dark vapor, or chill blast arise;
Seen all its lustre, all its sweetness fly,
Just wak'd to life, to charm—and then to die.

TO APATHY.

COME Apathy, come, steel my suffering heart,
Nor let it for another's sorrows heave;
Thy leaden wand to me O! but impart,
Then may my bosom haply cease to grieve.

When sorrow fills another's moisten'd eye,
When bursting anguish rends another's mind,
Let not my sullen heart responsive sigh,
Nor let them from my lips one comfort find.

Let me with stagnant eye their woes survey;
Survey the scalding tear bedew their cheek;
And thus with chilling coldness, simply say,
" Is it for me thou comfort com'st to seek ?"

But hold! tho' Apathy may sorrow less,
Does it e'er taste of pure unsulli'd joy?
No! it can ne'er like warmest feelings bless;
For we must suffer, or we can't enjoy.

ON CANDOR.

FAIR Candor, in thy pure unsullied mien,
Firm truth is ever most resplendent seen.
Smiling secure, thy spotless form we trace,
Lending a charm that wakes a new-born grace.
No coward mystery can a refuge find
Within the precincts of the candid mind ;
Scorning all mean disguise, all well-feign'd fear,
Seeming still more to know, than meets the ear.
Behold the empty head with secret great,
Whispering with caution, as if big with fate ;
Telling a nothing, with a pompous air,
And seeming sad with an ideal care.
Hence ! hated mystery, nor dare advance
With poisonous whisper, and with eye askance,
Sowing rank weeds within the human breast,
Which with fair Candor's flame should be
     possess'd.
No ! let pure Candor on the virtuous head
All its clear lustre in full radiance shed ;
And in the heart with truth be still enthron'd,
Pure thought, which may with confidence be
   - own'd.

D   THE

THE SOLDIER's GRAVE,

A SONG.

O! ne'er can sorrow's sacred tear
So well become a Briton's eye,
As when a Soldier's honor'd bier
Demands the glittering drop, the sigh.
For who like him from home remov'd,
Exposed upon the embattl'd plain,
Such glorious, dangerous toil has proved,
And there lies nobly slain.

For him who leaves his native shore
To meet the fateful shaft of death,
And mid the Battle's deafning roar
Resigns his ling'ring, parting, breath:
There blooms (when war's loud din is done)
A wreath of fair, of lasting fame,
To deck the Grave of valor's son;
To grace his honor'd name.

RESIGNA-

RESIGNATION.

HOW blest those hours which once I knew
When each fair day with gladness flew
Nor felt this heart a pain.
Of health, of wealth, of peace possess'd,
No racking thought within this breast
A refuge could obtain.

But now how alter'd is my fate!
How chang'd alas! my present state
From that e'er-while so blest;
Remov'd from those I fondly lov'd,
Depriv'd of all those joys I've prov'd,
Of health, of wealth, of rest!

And ah! within this sorrowing breast
A grief there lies so deep imprest
Which time can never heal;
No cure alas! can e'er be found
For pangs in dark concealment bound,
Pangs I can ne'er reveal.

Yet hold fond wretch, nor dare complain.
Dare not with murmurs to arraign
The wise decrees of God;
But to his Providence Divine
The good and ill of Life resign.
Submit—and kiss the rod.

WRITTEN

WRITTEN IN STOKE PARK.

STOKE, as thy beauteous scenes among
Pensive I tune my humble song;
As o'er thy velvet lawns I tread
With devious step by fancy led;
Or 'neath thy oaks impervious shade,
By winding stream or flowery glade,
Musing on all thy Owner's worth,
His polish'd manners, noble birth,
I pause ! with gratitude of heart
O'er-charg'd,—and thus my thoughts impart.—
But ah ! how impotent, how weak
My feeble strains, his praise to speak.
Yet hence vain fears, nor check my muse,
For he will surely not refuse,
With meek-eyed pity, mercifully kind,
This little leaf mid brighter bays to bind.

ON

ON READING SOME LINES

WRITTEN BY

JOHN PENN, Esq.

AND has that feeling heart e'er been distress'd ?
Has fate, untoward fate, e'er griev'd thy breast,
Where every Heav'n-born virtue warmly glows,
Whence mild benevolence unceasing flows?
Surely if merit could protect the heart
From woe-worn care's alas ! too fatal dart,
Thou had'st been safe,—nor should pale sorrow's
  sigh
Have heav'd thy breast, or tears have dimm'd thine
  Eye.
But ah ! 'tis not to erring mortals given
To scan the wise decrees of wondrous Heaven.
Nor let us murmur tho' they seem unjust.
Firm be our *Faith*, immovable our trust,
Our faith our trust in Providence divine ;
And to high Heaven each good and ill resign.

LINES ADDRESSED

TO

JOHN PENN, Esq.

TO foster Genius in its humble shed,
To mark where rests the long-forgotten dead,
To wipe the tear from penury's sad eye,
To sooth the sorrowing heart, to check the sigh,
Be thine;—but say to whom the power is given,
The wond'rous power, to speak thy praise ?—
    to Heaven.
To mighty Heaven then be the task resign'd;
For none on Earth can paint thy God-like mind.

ON LEAVING STOKE.

'MID scenes like these forever could I stray,
From grey-ey'd morn till evening's parting ray.
Mark ev'ry passing season's gradual change,
Nor form a thought, or breathe a wish to range.
But ah! alas! I'm destin'd to depart
From scenes that charm, that fascinate the heart.
Yet e'er I from these much-loved shades retire,
Let me once more with rapture strike the lyre.
O! beauteous *Stoke,* when first thy lawns I trac'd,
By classic taste improv'd, by nature grac'd,
This sorrowing heart a deep-drawn anguish griev'd;
With frequent sighs this hapless bosom heav'd.
But mild benevolence with eye serene,
And Heav'n-born friendship's sun-illum'd mien,
Beam'd o'er my soul, and cheer'd my aching heart;
Wak'd it to joy, and bid pale care depart;
Those nice attentions of the feeling mind,
That never flow but from that source refin'd,
Felt, *strongly felt,* but not to be express'd;
The first best balm to sooth the soul to rest.
Oh! then while memory in this bosom reigns,
Long as life's vital current fills these veins,
Thy worth shall live within this grateful breast,
" In Adamantine characters impress'd."

ON MY SISTER's BIRTHDAY.

JOY to thee, dear MATILDA! on this Day
Far be each pensive thought, each care, away!
May every passing year more brightly shine,
And every Earthly blessing still be thine!
Yes dearest girl, may all thy future hours
Be crown'd with pleasure's never-fading flowers:
Yet *we* ere-while have felt keen sorrow's dart
Pierce the remote recesses of the heart;
Felt the full force of poverty's chill wind,
In icy fetters each sensation bind.
But let us not complain, for has not Heav'n
Friends! O! *much valued friends*, in mercy given?
" Snatch'd from our Lips the chalice of despair,"
" And placed the cup of peace and plenty there?"

YES

YES, I have heard the sad, the bitter sigh.
The salt-tear oft has fill'd my pensive eye.
I've felt the force of disappointment's dart
Pierce the remote recesses of my heart.
Ah! I have felt ingratitude's fell sting,
Each fibre of my heart intensely wring.
Long lingring months of absence I have griev'd;
And where I *trusted most*, was *most deceived*.
But did this bosom ne'er that anguish know,
Which conscious guilt inflicts (severest woe!)
Ne'er has deception's mask disgrac'd my name;
Nor has dishonor dared approach my fame.
All, all but that the human heart may bear;
Guiltless and self approv'd, each minor ill may
    dare.

E   *HOPELESS*

HOPELESS LOVE.

Written at the request of a Friend.

WHY thus, ah ! why, while gazing on that face,
Feels my sad heart this sickning sense of pain ?
Why, as those features I minutely trace,
My starting tears I scarcely can restrain ?

Ah ! why alas ! when thou art haply near,
Why does my breast so struggle with a sigh ?
Why do I trembling thus with doubt and fear
Cast to the earth my pensive, timid eye ?

Why, as that dulcet voice I lean to hear,
Why does such chilling anguish seize my heart ?
Why from that smile do I a mischief fear
Which to each other does a joy impart ?

Alas ! the fatal cause too well I know ;
Know but too well the misery of my state ;
Feel the full force of each impending woe,
Yet have not courage to avoid my fate.

Thus oft we see an insect madly dare,
With ventrous wing, amid'st consuming fires ;
Hov'ring around the taper's vivid glare,
Till in the flame it sinks, and sad expires.

THE

THE BEGGAR GIRL,

A SONG.

The first and second Verses written by a Gentleman, the third by me.

OVER the Mountains, and over the Moor,
Barefoot and hungry I wander forlorn.
My father is dead, and my mother is poor;
And she grieves for the days that can never re-
    turn.
Pity ye kind-hearted friends of humanity.
Cold blows the wind and the night's coming on.
Give me some food for my mother in charity.
Give me some food, and then I'll begone.

Think, while ye revel so careless and free,
Secure from the blast and well cloathed and fed,
Should fortune so change it, how hard it would be,
To beg at a door for a morsel of bread.
Pity ! ye kind-hearted *Friends* of humanity.
Cold blows the wind, and the night's coming on.
Give me some food for my mother in charity.
Give me some food, and then I'll begone.

Thanks generous stranger, so gentle, so fair;
How beauteous thou look'st while thus ye bestow!

How

How blest thy sensations to drive away care,
To make the heart glad and the tear cease to flow!
Thanks gen'rous, *kind-hearted friend* of *humanity*.
Tho' cold blows the wind and night's coming on;
We shall have food by your bounty, your charity.
We shall have food, and with blessings I'm gone.

ON

ON FRIENDSHIP.

FRIENDSHIP, thou pure tho' prostituted name,
Thy genuine feelings O! how few can claim!
How many use the sacred name of friend,
Professing much to serve some selfish end!
When we the thorny couch of sickness press,
When the torn heart is wounded with distress,
When the bright sunshine of our hope is gone,
When all the flattering smiles of fortune flown,
Then, then we see *true friendship* stand confess'd,
The fairest virtue in the human breast.——
Waked by its soothing voice, a chearing ray
Will round the heart an instant haply play.
Charm'd by its power, the sorrowing breast may
    feel
A transitory touch of joy within it steal.—
O! *I have* felt its powerful influence kind
Shed its soft balm thro' my distracted mind.
Have seen fell anguish at its presence fly,
While misery's power has ceased to force the sigh,
O! blessed good, in mercy kindly given,
Fore-taste on Earth of all we hope in Heaven,
O! true, O! generous friendship, in thy balm,
The ruffled soul enjoys a transient calm.
Hush'd are its stormy passions into rest,
And peaceful queit lulls the troubled breast.
Let me ne'er cease thy precious stream to sip!
Thy nectar'd cup O! dash not from my lip!

For

For in the healing draught we surely find
Solace for every ill that wounds the mind.
O! may'st thou still around my heart entwine
Thy fairest wreath! *true* friendship, still be mine!
Let not insidious envy, baleful weed,
'Mongst its sweet flowers destroying poisons breed,
To blight the cherish'd plant; while malice dire
Withers each bud, and all its charms expire.
No! rather let it live its longest day;
Leave it its power to chace pale care away;
Still let it Monarch reign within my heart;
Still to my griefs its sovereign balm impart.
Friendship can smooth the thorny couch of care;
Can almost lull the pangs of keen despair;
Rob e'en the shaft of death of half its smart,
And bid the trembling soul in peace depart.
Its *sterling worth* I've prov'd,—and I have seen
Its *countefeit*,—apeing its Heaven-born mien;
To cheat the open unsuspecting mind,
And in deceit's fell toils, sensation bind;
Till fickle fortune's sudden frown has prov'd
The *emptiness* of what seem'd worthy to be lov'd.

SONNET.

SONNET.

WHEN virtue's radiant beam we clearly trace
In every movement of the feeling heart;
When her pure rays illume the expressive face,
And to the form her Heaven-born charms impart;
What wonder if while gazing on that form
The heart be captive taken, or that I
Poor thoughtless maid, unconscious of all harm,
Should, as I wond'ring gaze, thus hopeless sigh?
Yet am I proud to own thy sov'reign power;
Prouder to estimate each worth aright.
This soothing thought will cheer my latest hour,
And fill my soul with pure unmix'd delight.
Are we not taught fair virtue's form to love ?
Yes, and where virtue's shines, 'tis virtue to approve.

Written

Written after seeing the Room at Ranelagh, *that was*
built for the Fete given by BOODLE's *Club.*

FILL'D with delight and wonder, while we rove
Thro' the bright mazes of the enchanting grove;
Behold from bough to bough, by magic powers
Suspended, shine festoons of fiery flowers!
Or see amid th' illumin'd branches shoot
The crimson lustre of Hesperian fruit.
Shut from the cheering ray and fresh'ning gale,
The native hues of vegetation fail;
And ev'ry weeping hamadryad sees
In silent woe, her fate-devoted trees.
So, when from rural shades and rural air
To midnight revels flies the blooming fair,
Tho' all the toilet's varied stores combine
To add new graces to a form divine,
Transient and weak is art's pernicious aid;
Soon the pure charms of genuine nature fade;
Health's liquid radiance quits her languid eyes;
And on her cheek the rose of beauty dies.

WRITTEN AT STOKE PARK,

AUGUST *the 6th.* 1802.

HOW blissful pass these truely happy hours,
My path thus strew'd with friendship's hallow'd
flowers !
Could I but check these moments as they fly !
Too swiftly yet alas ! I heave a sigh,
Thinking, so fares it with our every joy,
While pain and care such tedious hours employ.
But let me not ungratefully complain,
Nor dim my present joy by future pain.
No; rather let me while these moments last
Think of no ill to come, no sorrows past;
For surely 'tis a cheering ray from Heaven,
To dry the bitter tears I've shed, in mercy given.

SONG.

SONG.

*Written on the Idea that real Love is not a selfish
Passion in the Female Heart, after having had a
Dispute on the Subject with a Gentleman.*

HOPELESS alas! I gaze on that lov'd form;
Hopeless alas! I hear those accents mild;
Hopeless alas! behold that beauteous smile,
Which oft my bosom's anguish hath beguil'd.

A happier maid shall gaze on that lov'd form;
A happier maid shall those soft accents hear;
A happier maid behold that beauteous smile,
While I in absence sigh, and drop the tear.

Yet wherefore sigh, and wherefore drop the tear?
If he be blest, ah! why should I repine?
Selfish that heart which owns another wish;
For sure his happiness must still be mine.

LINES

LINES ADDRESSED

TO

JOHN PENN, Esq.

On his Birthday, February, 1802.

O!, had I all the winning grace of speech,
All the vast power of eloquence divine,
With fervent prayer high Heav'n I would beseech
That ev'ry earthly blessing should be thine.
That, on this morn which brings thy natal hour,
Aurora's gates should ope with brighter ray ;
That ev'ry plant should bear a sweeter flower,
To hail this sacred, this auspicious day.
That each revolv'ing year serene might fly,
And bring thee nought but pleasure in its train ;
That no unhappiness should cause a sigh,
And that thy heart should never feel a pain.
Alas ! such prayers are unavailing all ;
For frail mortality is doom'd to grieve.
Still we must sigh, and tears alas ! must fall ;
And we must sorrow 'till we cease to live.
But when within the breast glows virtue rare,
Such as in thine, we may defy each Earth-born
    care.

ADDRESSED TO STOKE PARK,

Under the painful Idea of not seeing it again.

O! beauteous STOKE, so much, so justly lov'd;
Where I ere-while a transient respite prov'd
From sorrow's piercing sting, from cruel woe;
And where awhile my tears forgot to flow;
O! much-lov'd STOKE, shall I alas! no more
Thy verdant lawns, thy shadowy groves, explore?
No more at early dawn with lightsome pace
Thy dew-bespangled glades shall I retrace?
No more, as setting sol's declining rays
Throw o'er thy woods a rich resplendent blaze,
Shall I, with calm unruffl'd soul, retire,
Thankful of heart, and grateful strike the lyre?
Ah! no! it will not be! 'twas bliss too vast,
Too dazzling bright those days, and fair, to last.
And ah! too slightly valued, while possess'd,
Those happy hours replete with peace, with rest.
Yet, tho' they 're fled, ah! never to return;
Tho' I alas! their flight must ceaseless mourn,
Treasur'd in faithful memory they'll remain,
And solace lend to each succeeding pain.

SONG,

SONG,

Altered and added to.

TO thy peace hapless maiden adieu
And adieu every joy thou hast known;
Thy joys, like the rose in the morning that blows,
But e'er noon all its blossoms are flown.
Forget each kind sentence ye heard,
Forget each soft hope, and each strain;
Thy strain is neglected, and dead is thy hope,
But ye never shall hear me complain.

'Tis for her who still hopes, to complain;
To complain of the coldness she fears;
But to her who is chill'd by despair
No solace is found but in tears.
No! from Laura's sad lip a reproach
Shall ne'er flow to accuse her lov'd friend;
And tho' her heart bursts with despair,
To complain shall her mind ne'er descend.

TO LADY JANE ASTON.

MARK in her speaking eye fair truth express'd,
See the pure lilly blooming on her breast;
Within that breast each virtue is inshrin'd
With all good grace, to grace the female mind.
Firm in her friendship, worthy to be lov'd,
An ornament to ev'ry state she's prov'd.
Open, ingenuous, quite devoid of art,
Pure thoughts spontaneous flowing from her heart.
But ah! how feeble are my humble lays
To speak her virtues, or attempt her praise!
Yet friendship with kind pity will excuse
This trifling tribute of my trembling muse.

LINES

LINES WRITTEN

On passing a very happy Day at CLIFDEN *Spring,*
August the 13*th.* 1802.

WHY doth the trickling tear bedew my cheek?
Ah! wherefore doth my heart, untoward, sigh?
Why thus, ah! why, unconscious do I seek
The shade, and from society thus fly?

Surely each happiness, each joy is mine,
By friendship shelter'd, and by friendship bless'd;
Why then, ah! why, ungratefully thus pine?
Why let this seeming anguish fill my breast?

'Tis not from grief alone that tears will flow;
Nor is it grief alone that prompts the sigh.
Fullness of bliss will, equally with woe,
Heave the swoln heart, and fill the pensive eye,

———————

Come Ladies, here's a Heart to win,
Most amply stored with worth within ;
Yet to attain it, ye will find
A puzzle to perplex the mind.
But come 'tis worth your while to try,
Nor let the blessing past ye fly.

So stor'd with Judgment is the Head
That guides the Breast by reason led,
That t'will require an able dart
To touch this firm, this guarded Heart.
Happy the maid who wins the Prize!
Her *Purse* must gain it, *not her Eyes.*

F I N I S.